LET'S
DISCOVER

CHURCHES

Charles Bradley

W

Schools Library and Information Services

FF

© Franklin Watts 1993
This edition: 2002

Franklin Watts
96 Leonard Street
London EC2A 4XD

Franklin Watts Australia
56 O'Riordan Street
Alexandria, Sydney, NSW 2015

ISBN: 0 7496 4572 5 (pbk)

Dewey Decimal Classification: 726

A CIP catalogue record for this book is
available from the British Library

Editor: Sarah Ridley
Designer: Janet Watson
Photographer: Chris Fairclough
Picture researcher: Joanne King
Consultant: Hal Bishop

Additional photographs: courtesy of the
Aldeburgh Festival Foundation 9b; Bridgeman
Art Library 6t; Collections 7br, 11t, 26t; et
archive 5c, 11bl, 11br; Robert Harding Picture
Library 7bl, 27t; Sonia Halliday 21tl; Michael
Holford 5t, 7tl, 7tr, 9t, 21bl; many thanks to
Diana May, Joanna and Michael 13b; Ann and
Bury Peerless 5b; Bill Stephenson 8b.

Acknowledgements: the author and publishers
wish to thank Imogen Brown, G R Barclay and
Class 5 of St Michael's School, Aldbourne;
Peter Hyson, Vicar, and the Churchwardens of
St Michael's, Aldbourne for their help and
support in producing this book.

Printed in Malaysia

Contents

Looking at places of worship

Churches can be found throughout the world, wherever there are Christians. They are the Christian place of worship and are often the biggest buildings in the local area. Many are built on slightly higher ground than surrounding buildings — their tall bell towers visible from afar.

People of other faiths have also constructed impressive places of worship. Moslems use mosques whilst Hindus worship in temples, Sikhs in gurdwaras and Jews in synagogues.

Many churches are very old and provide an excellent source of history for a local community. By looking at details of their architecture it is usually possible to tell when they were built. Inside the church there are often many clues about the people who have worshipped there.

LET'S INVESTIGATE

Today the population of Britain includes people from many different cultures. Find out what religions people profess in your area, and what sorts of buildings they use for their worship.

The ancient Greeks worshipped many gods. This temple at the Acropolis, Athens was dedicated to Nike, the goddess of victory.

St Michael's Church, the church featured in this book, towers over the village of Aldbourne in Wiltshire.

Moslems worship in a mosque. Five times a day, a muezzin's voice summons Moslems to prayer from the top of a tall minaret.

Jewish people use a synagogue as their place of worship. The Ark of the Covenant, where the Torah (holy scrolls) is kept, is the holiest part of the synagogue.

5

What are churches made from?

The earliest Christians in Britain built churches from timber. Timber does not last well in a damp climate and, after a time, rots away. So, only one example of an Anglo-Saxon wooden church remains in Britain today. The Anglo-Saxons also used stone for their churches, such as at Bradford-upon Avon, Wiltshire, but it was not until after the Norman Conquest, in 1066, that the use of stone became widespread.

However, large areas of Britain lack suitable building stone. This meant that stone had to be transported long distances, sometimes even from abroad, to build a church. Where there is a good local building stone, you may find churches looking similar.

When a village wanted to build a new church it chose a master mason, who prepared the design, arranged for the labour and selected the materials.

This picture is taken from a 15th century manuscript and shows stone masons at work building a cathedral.

The master carpenter went into the nearby wood or forest to choose the wood for scaffolding and for the ceiling and church interior.

LET'S INVESTIGATE

Look at a geological map of your area. What is the most common sort of stone? Find out whether it has been quarried and how the stone has been used.

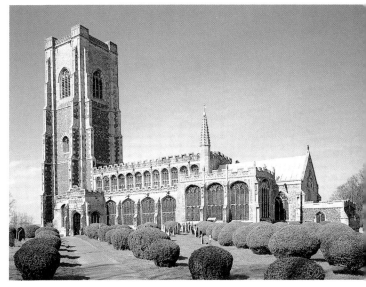

The Anglo-Saxon wooden church at Greenstead-juxta-Ongar, Essex is the only surviving example of an early wooden church. The chancel, built of brick, was added c.1500.

The size of a church often reflects how wealthy the community was. The people of Lavenham, Suffolk, were wealthy in the Middle Ages through their production of wool and were able to build this impressive church.

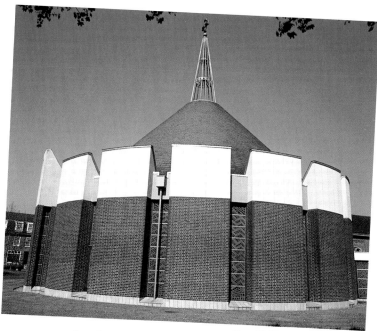

Brick was used to build churches from the 15th century onwards. Many churches built during the Victorian period, such as this London church, used brick.

In the last century, new building materials have become available to church builders. St Mary's Church at Hatfield is built of a mixture of brick, steel and concrete.

The uses of the Church, past and present

In the Middle Ages, the Church and its officials were very powerful. Bishops lived in palaces and controlled the local churches within an area known as a diocese. The Church had great influence over everyone's lives.

Apart from its use as a place of worship, a church was also used for other activities. It sometimes became a market place, or a group of travelling players might perform a mystery play there. The church could also provide emergency shelter at times of need. In the latter part of the 18th century there were two great fires in Aldbourne and the church provided shelter for the homeless.

In some churches where there was a room over the porch, it was used as a schoolroom for local children. In the Middle Ages, when few people could read, the church building itself taught people stories from the Bible through paintings on the walls or stained glass windows.

Justice was often administered and fines and taxes collected by church officials. The church was used as a place from which to make announcements. It was large enough for the whole village to gather. In times of unrest, men might be called to the church to join the local army.

Mystery plays are still performed in some cities and towns. These plays are based on religious stories and were originally performed on holidays in the Middle Ages.

This 13th century wall painting at the Church of St Peter and St Paul, Chaldon, Surrey, gave a strong message to the local worshippers. The saved are shown climbing the ladder to Heaven whilst the damned descend into Hell, where demons hurl them onto the fire.

Now churches are often used for concerts or dramatic performances. Many people can be seated in the pews and enjoy the beautiful surroundings at the same time as the entertainment.

9

A short history of Christianity in Britain

A church can often reveal evidence of the history of Christianity in this country, depending on how old it is and how much it has been restored.

Christianity was present in Roman Britain from around AD 200. Often the site used for an early form of worship became the place where a stone church was eventually built.

Up until the reign of Henry VIII (1509-1547), the English Church followed the authority of the Pope, head of the Church of Rome. However, when the Pope refused to grant Henry a divorce from his first wife, Catherine of Aragon, Henry broke with the Roman Church to gain his divorce. He declared himself head of the Church of England. This was the English Reformation.

The Reformation led to great changes in the Church of England as the church moved away from some of its traditions of worship. Rood screens dividing the people in the nave from the priest in the chancel were usually removed. Look for evidence of this. Some church monuments and wall paintings were destroyed or mutilated to make the churches more simple.

There are various historical sources that may refer to your church. There may be a guide book that tells you about its history or a local expert on the church. Look through local history books to find out about your church.

These statues were mutilated by Puritans, a religious group, who destroyed many forms of decoration in churches around the country.

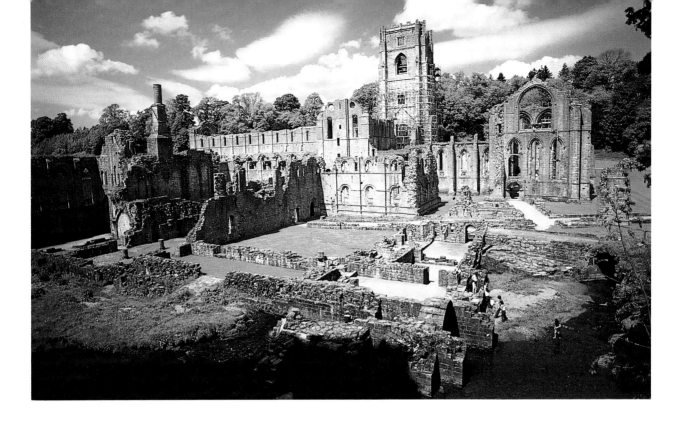

When Henry VIII broke with the Roman Church, he also dissolved the monasteries. The monks were sent away and the buildings stripped of their wealth and sold. The roof was removed from Fountains Abbey, Yorkshire, so it gradually fell into ruins.

William the Conqueror (1066-87) ordered a grand survey of property owners to be made, called the Domesday Book. It was completed in 1086. Find out if your church is mentioned in it.

Saint Augustine became the first Archbishop of Canterbury when he re-established links between the English and Roman Catholic Churches.

People involved with the church

A vicar, rector or curate, is in charge of a parish, or parishes, in his local area. He conducts services in the church, christens, marries and buries people, visits the sick and comforts people in distress, as well as being involved in many community activities.

The vicar is helped in this work by many people. Churchwardens and sidesmen hand out service sheets and hymn books and administer the collection. Other people organise a rota of flower-decorating and cleaning of the church, so that it always looks beautiful on Sundays. The organist plays the hymns and rehearses the choir, and bell ringers ring the bells.

The Church holds many different services through the year. Christmas is the time when the birth of Jesus is celebrated, whilst at Easter the story of his crucifixion and resurrection are commemorated.

Interview your local vicar about his work in the community.

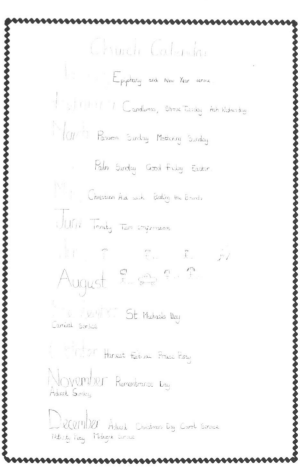

Find out about some of the important dates in the Christian year.

LET'S INVESTIGATE

Vicars make sure that the churches in their parish are looked after. They often have local help. Find out how many people are involved in your church. Discover what they do and how often they do it.

Volunteers at St Michael's come to clean the church once a week.

Two villagers regularly tidy the graveyard.

Others clean the brass.

Joanne and Matthew were married at St Michael's. Marriages are times of great happiness when a couple choose to pledge themselves to each other in front of friends and relatives.

13

Approaching the church

Most churches are surrounded by a wall containing consecrated, or holy, ground where people are buried. The graveyard which surrounds the church is often a haven for wild flowers and some wild animals, because herbicides are not normally used and the area is quite undisturbed. It is possible to find all sorts of plants growing there which are no longer found elsewhere locally. Yew was once thought to be the only tree that could grow in soil containing dead bodies, but there are often other types of trees to be found.

These are some of the plants and wildlife found in the graveyard at Aldbourne. An area has been set aside as a wildlife sanctuary.

church with tower   church with spire   no tower or spire

Churches are important landmarks. They are depicted on ordnance survey maps by several symbols. Look at the ordnance survey map for your area to locate your local church.

In the churchyard, use a compass to find out which end of the church faces east.

Look at the inscriptions on the gravestones and find out how old people were when they died. Before this century, many women died giving birth and babies were often taken ill and died before their second birthday.

The earliest graves were marked with a simple wooden board, but these have long since disappeared. People then started to use engraved slabs of stone, similar to the stone used to build the church. In the Georgian period (1714-1830) some families built large vaults where all the family could eventually be buried. Modern headstones are often made from polished marble.

Consecrated land around the church has always been limited for space and graves can be redug after 100 years or so. The old headstones are removed and are often used for paving paths or are propped up against the church.

The grave on the right of this picture is a Georgian chest tomb. It lies over a vault, containing the graves of several members of one family.

Graves have been marked with different shaped gravestones over the years.

Over the years, the rain and wind may wear away the inscriptions on the grave-stones.

Look around the churchyard to find out why people died, and how old they were at death.

Looking at the outside of the church

Churches were often built over a long period of time and in a variety of styles. The shape of the windows and doors gives a clue to the age of the church.

There are other ways to work out how old a church is. If it has a short solid tower, it is likely to be from the Norman period (1060s-1180s). If it has a tall, elegant tower or pointed spire, it is possibly from the Gothic period (1180s-1540), although a church's spire has often been added later.

Other features of the Gothic style are pointed arches, flying buttresses and ribbed vaults. This style of architecture developed over a period of 300 years.

During the Norman period, churches were built using semi-circular arches. These were similar to those of the ancient Romans so this style is known as Romanesque.

In the Gothic period, there was a desire for churches to let in more light. Many churches were altered to insert a row of windows high above the nave. This is called the clerestory.

In the 17th century, some churches were built in a Classical style of architecture, imitating the decoration and types of columns and capitals from the classical world of the ancient Greeks and Romans.

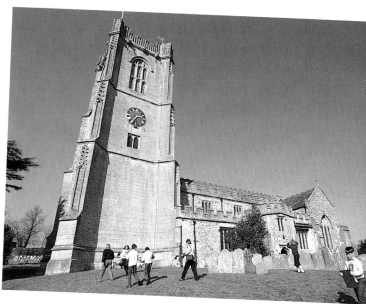

This pointed arch is typical of the Gothic style. Always look at the shape of the arches used in windows and doors when you are trying to work out when a church was built.

Look at the outside of your local church to see how many different styles of architecture you can find.

Stone masons sometimes expressed their individuality by carving grotesque heads in the stone work. Some of these heads are called gargoyles as they are adapted to act as water spouts, carrying water away from the walls at roof level.

17

Inside the church

A church is divided into different areas, not all of which have walls around them. The porch is at the entrance to the church. People used to use this room to swear solemn and binding oaths for business. Sometimes there was a room over the porch which might be used as a schoolroom or even as a place for a priest to live in. Today notices about parish business are put on the porch notice board.

The central part of the church is known as the nave. This is where the congregation sits. On one or both sides of the nave in larger churches, there may be a north and south aisle. The aisle acts as an extension to the nave and is used when the church is very full. Coming off the nave at right-angles are the transepts which make the church plan into the shape of a cross. Transepts were added to provide extra space either side of the altar.

At the east end of the nave is the chancel, where the altar with its cross is placed. It is here that a vicar conducts services. On either side of the chancel or nave there may be chapels. Chantry chapels were built by wealthy families while other chapels were often built by craftsmen's guilds and dedicated to their patron saint.

In St Michael's, the nave is filled with pews for the congregation. It usually forms the biggest area of the church.

The high window above the door of the south porch at St Michael's shows that there was once a room here.

This chapel was built by the Waldronds who were an important local family in Aldbourne.

The vestry is the vicar's private room where he changes into the vestments that he wears to conduct a service. Here, too, he keeps the register for births and marriages, and stores valuable church objects in a safe.

Measure out your church by pacing it out, and draw a plan. Mark the position of the doors, windows and other features. You might find that the plan makes the shape of the cross, the symbol of Christianity.

Special features in the church

All churches have specialised furniture for church functions. The font is used at Christening services when babies or young people are baptised in to the Church for the first time. Water is poured into the font and blessed. A small amount of water is used to make the sign of the Christian cross on the child's head.

The pulpit stands to one side of the nave, looking down towards the pews. Here the vicar delivers his sermon. Towards the end of the 17th century, when there was so much new thinking in religion, sermonising became very important. The vicar might talk for over an hour.

Near the pulpit there is often a large bookstand called a lectern, on which the Holy Bible sits. This is the most sacred book of Christianity. People read from the Bible during services.

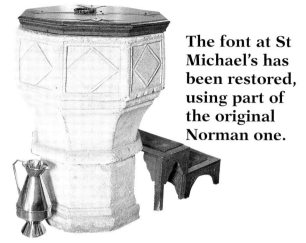

The font at St Michael's has been restored, using part of the original Norman one.

This Jacobean pulpit was brought to St Michael's from another church in the 19th century. The same architect was restoring both churches.

Sometimes you will find a hole in the wall of a chapel to allow the people present inside to see the vicar at vital moments in the service. This hole is called a squint.

Churches did not always have places to sit. It was not until the 18th century that pews became common, although many churches had benches around the outside walls of the church earlier than this. Rich families in Georgian times had their own private box pews built. The high-sided seats hid the family from general view. Many of the pews in churches today were put in during the reign of Queen Victoria (1837-1901).

Wealthy Georgians paid rent to the church for the box pews they sat in.

Some churches and cathedrals still contain medieval pews. This beautifully carved pew end is at Salisbury Cathedral.

If your church has a memorial brass, ask permission to take a brass rubbing. Tape some strong, thin paper over the brass. Feel the outline of the brass underneath and carefully rub over it with a wax crayon. Always rub in the same direction.

Music and the Church

Music has always played an important part in the Church. The Church commissioned composers to write music especially for its services, and continues to do so. Much of this music has become well-known outside the Church.

Originally all Church music was sung with no accompaniment. It evolved from pre-Christian chanting. By the time of Henry VIII's split with Rome, long and complicated masses were being performed in churches. Hymns and psalms took over from the mass as a way to involve the people more in the service.

These children are performing a hymn that they have written.

Many churches have bells hanging in the tower. The loft where they are kept is called the belfry and there are slits in the stone to let the sound out. The huge brass bells are connected to ropes which hang down inside the tower, right to the ground. Here bellringers can ring the bells to summon people to services.

Write your own hymn. Either set it to a tune you already know or make up your own tune.

Some of the bells in St Michael's were cast at the bell foundry that used to exist in the village. Each bell is a different weight and size and so makes a slightly different sound.

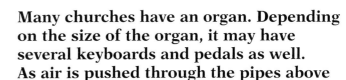

Many churches have an organ. Depending on the size of the organ, it may have several keyboards and pedals as well. As air is pushed through the pipes above the keyboard, a sound comes out. The sound can be altered by pulling out a variety of 'stops' called names such as the Flute, the Grand Bass and the Choir.

Memorials and artefacts

If you look carefully at the floors and the walls and investigate all the dark corners of a church, you can find all sorts of interesting things. Sometimes there are engraved stone slabs in the floor or memorial tablets on the wall which tell of some eminent person lying underneath. Families had to pay for the privilege of burying their relatives inside the church. These burials took place until 1854 when an act of Parliament put a stop to the custom. It was considered unhygenic to have bodies decomposing inside the building.

Behind this door in St Michael's was the old staircase that went up to a room over the porch (see page 18). It is now blocked at the top.

One of the two 18th century fire engines kept in St Michael's. This one is called Adam and its smaller partner, Eve. They have been placed in the church to keep them safe.

This monument is in one of the chapels at St Michael's. It is thought to show Richard Goddard, who died in 1615, his wife and four children.

These two war memorials recall the men of Aldbourne killed in the two World Wars.

Sometimes there is a list of the vicars that have served in the church. The first vicar recorded on this board is Richard de Whityngdigh in 1301. The church was reconsecrated to St Michael in 1460 – previously it had been St Mary's.

The monarch is the head of the Church of England. Royal patronage is often shown by a coat-of-arms. This is the coat-of-arms of Queen Anne (1702-1714).

Stained glass windows

As very few people were able to read in the Middle Ages, the Church used stained glass windows to relate the stories of the Bible and important messages of Church teaching. Sometimes the windows were also built as a memorial to an important figure or event.

Stained glass is still made today. This is a modern window in the church at St Agnes on the Scilly Isles.

This stained glass window at St Michael's shows the crucifixion of Christ.

Stained glass was very popular from the 12th century onwards. Fragments of glass were held together with H-shaped metal bars called cames. Coloured glass was the most highly-prized and expensive type available, so often clear glass was used. Each little piece of glass was then individually painted with enamel to build up the desired picture or pattern.

Stained glass was removed from churches and many buildings during the Second World War (1939-1945) to save it from being damaged by bombs.

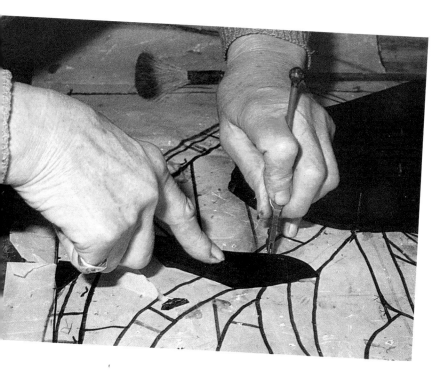

A modern stained glass maker cuts out the glass, using the template design he created earlier.

Make a stained glass window using black card and coloured tissue paper. Choose a theme and draw a design on the card in white crayon. Carefully cut out the design. Glue coloured tissue over the cut-outs.

This window was made by children and shows the story of the Creation.

Making guides to your church

Many churches have some sort of guide which you can buy, but they are mostly for adults. With all the information that you have discovered, make a guide to your church for other children to use.

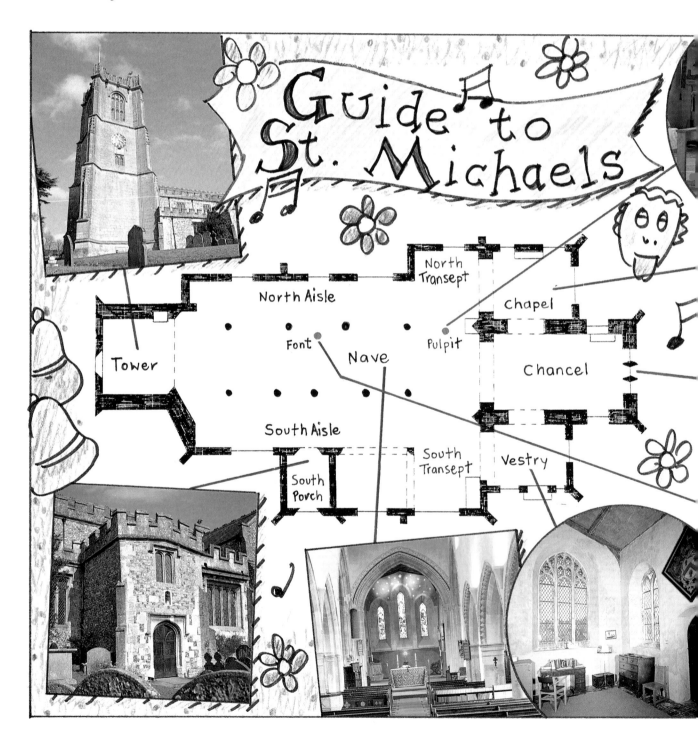

Guide to St. Michaels

North Transept

North Aisle

Chapel

Tower

Font

Pulpit

Nave

Chancel

South Aisle

South Porch

South Transept

Vestry

One way to do this would be to make a plan of your church, showing all the different areas. Then add drawings or photos of all the features, so that the reader can see what the church looks like.

Video guide

It is not always possible to visit other churches or places of worship far away. You could make a video guide to your church, like these children did, which you could exchange with another school or church.

Making a video needs careful planning. First you need to write a script, then you need to choose a presenter who will read the story while a camera person films around the church. You will need to arrange and carry out interviews with some of the people involved in the church. Finally, ask your teacher to help you edit the final version of the guide so that it is ready to watch.

When filming round the church, try to get some interesting angles and use the zoom, if there is one.

More things to do

Gargoyle masks

Make a gargoyle mask by pasting glue and newspaper over one half of a blown-up balloon. When the newspaper has dried, remove the balloon and cut holes for your eyes and mouth. Paint it in gruesome colours. Fix a length of elastic on to the mask so that you can wear it.

The saint comic strip

Most churches are dedicated to a particular saint. Find out the history of the saint your church is dedicated to. Draw a comic strip of his or her life.

Glossary

ARK OF THE COVENANT
A tabernacle or cupboard in a synagogue, usually in the eastern wall, for the TORAH scrolls. The Ark is symbolic of God's presence amongst the Israelites on their journey from Egypt to the Promised Land of Canaan.

CAPITAL
Upper part of a column from which an arch or vaulting rib may spring.

CHANTRY CHAPEL
Chapel endowed for the singing of masses for the soul of the founder and his family in the pre-Reformation period.

DISSOLUTION OF THE MONASTERIES
Henry VIII's dispossession of the monastic orders, their wealth and property between 1538-40. This occured as a result of his break with the Church of Rome, necessary to obtain a divorce from his first wife, Catherine of Aragon.

FLYING BUTTRESS
Buttress supporting a wall or other structure by an arch that spreads the load outwards and downwards.

GOTHIC
Dominant architectural style for most of the Middle Ages which flourished from 1180s to c.1540. The style is dominated by pointed arches, flying buttresses and ribbed vaults.

JACOBEAN
Of the time of King James 1 of England (VI of Scotland) 1603-25. Usually refers to the furniture style characterised by use of oak and panelling.

NORMAN
Architectural style dominant from the 1060s-1180s, characterised by round arches, massive walls, and columns and clasping buttresses.

PURITANS
Extreme English protestants who wished to 'purify' the Church of England of much of its ceremony and other residual elements of catholicism.

REFORMATION
The religious/political movement of 16th century Europe that began as an attempt to reform the Roman Catholic Church and resulted in the establishment of the protestant churches.

TORAH
The first five books of the Old Testament: Genesis, Exodus, Leviticus, Numbers and Deuteronomy.

VAULT
Arched structure forming a ceiling or roof.

Index